My Amazing Journey

Gloria D. Hazelwood

Papyrus Publishing Inc.
Brooklyn Park • Minnesota • USA

Hazelwood, Gloria D., *My Amazing Journey*

This publication was produced as part of Papyrus Publishing Inc.'s Heritage Preservation Project, which promotes and encourages our parents, grandparents and elders to share their wisdom, knowledge, history, heritage, customs and culture through multimedia publications in order to help preserve family and community continuity and to link our future generations to their past.

ISBN: 978-0-9882883-0-0

Papyrus Publishing Inc.
Brooklyn Park, Minnesota, United States of America
PapyrusPublishing@MSN.com

Dedication and Acknowledgements

To my family who I loved and lived for. I want to
acknowledge them as a part of my book. You are part of
"My Amazing Journey."

My Husband
John

My Son and Daughter
John (Patricia) and Brenda (Jackie)

My Grand Children
Jeremy, Janelle, Marcus, Matthew, Patrick, Leanna, Andrea,
Andrew, Daneen, Sherry, Robert

My Great Grand Child
Jere' Yonna

Contents

Foreword

My mother, Gloria, is an example of the importance of family. She lives for family. Her life is an example of a virtuous woman. She has always been a stable factor in my life. I would not be where I am if it wasn't for her steadfast love and care. She has the ability to create the kind of memories that make us laugh, reflect, and cause us to smile. I can only imagine what her thoughts and feelings were as a strong Army wife, traveling with two small children on a transatlantic ship to Europe to be with my father, who was on military tour. Even more so, while traveling on the ship with a child who had pneumonia, me! She has always exhibited so much love, grace, and a humble character for us to glean from. I love the fact that she has decided to create a family heirloom in the form of this book. I can hear her grandchildren talking already, "Remember when grandma said..." They say behind every good man is a great woman. Her commitment to maintain a strong marriage and close family is commendable. That's my mom, and I love her very much. I thank her again. My hope is that my children Jeremy, Janelle, Marcus, Matthew, Patrick, Leanna, Andrea, Andrew, and Daneen will carry on their family heritage by living a righteous and committed life before their family like their grandmother. She always made sure that her love for God and her trust in Him were highlighted through her many times of encouragement through tough times in life.

Lastly, I hope we all, each generation, will carry on the chapters of her book with their lives, their stories, and their trust in the Lord and on the journey that He takes them.

John E. Hazelwood, Jr., Son of Gloria Hazelwood

Preface

My life has been a journey in learning how to love myself and extending that love to others. I think back a moment, not just where I was born, but also the circumstances that contributed to my being here. No matter who we are, or where we live, we all have our own journey.

Mine began the moment I was born to LeRoy & Agnes Patterson at the hospital in Iowa City, Iowa. Since I was the fourth girl born, I wondered if they expected a boy at that time. I guess my mom said, "We have another girl, LeRoy." My birth was surrounded with happiness. I was born into a world where people lovingly greeted you and celebrated your arrival. In this book, I tell how my parents played a significant part in my life.

We are each responsible for our own life. Life is a series of all your experiences. It is a journey of learning to love. As far back as I can recall my prayer in church would be, "Use me God. Show me how to take who I am, who I want to be, and what I can do, and use it for a purpose greater than myself." This book is about my LIFE and PURPOSE.

I had the courage to follow my passion of what I wanted to do-and if you don't know what it is for you, realize that one reason for your existence on earth is to find it. Your life's work is to find it – and exercise the discipline, tenacity, and hard work it takes to pursue it.

In this book I share with you my purpose, and I share a sense of my history, heritage, philosophies, inner feelings, disappointments, and joys. I talk about Fort Dodge, Iowa, my birthplace. I talk about my five sisters, my husband, two children, 11 grandchildren, and my great-grandchild. This book first and foremost is for my family so they may continue building upon the foundation my parents laid for my sisters and me. This foundation has made me strong and confident. My husband and I have continued this work for our two children, and they are doing a great job in laying this foundation for their children. My wishes are for my grandchildren and great-grandchildren to continue this legacy of family, tradition, and God. This book is also for anyone who wishes to succeed in life. The stories in this book are examples of love, success, and commitment. There are stories of what you can have and be. Above all, this book shows how every one of us is important and necessary to God's plan. After reading my stories, you will have more faith and confidence in yourself. I have included those things that might help my family. The experiences that I have had throughout my travels have taught me about life. I have been guided by one major thing: LOVE! If that love comes through this book, then it was well worth the effort.

Gloria D. (Patterson) Hazelwood

Where I'm From

I'm from scrubbed kitchen floors and vegetable gardens,
From tupperware bowls demonstrating parties.

I'm from Coppin Chapel Church in Fort Dodge, Iowa with
Christmas time plays and music,
from melodies playing violin and piano.

I'm from mother's strong eyes, and Daddy's strong faith.

From five sisters to share our love with jokes,
laughter and constant chatter.

I'm from classrooms and boardrooms,
chalkboards and keyboards.

I'm from my son's and daughter's laughter and constant chatter.

From my husband's smiles and guidance to family and friends.

I'm from traveling by air and sea through Europe

and United States.

From Mary Kay's Go-Give spirit with courage and confidence.

We create from our past, but share in our future
certain to realize whatever we choose.

Let's go there together, let's laugh there together.
From the past to remember and the future we share
and live together in a beautiful creative moment.

I'm from all the moments remembered
by our generation with all the things we did,
and how we did them, with confidence and prayers.

Gloria

My Early Days in Historic Iowa
The Hawkeye State

"In this life we can do no great things, just small things with Great Love."

Mother Teresa

I've traveled throughout the United States and Europe, and I would always have someone ask me, "Where are you from?" I would say, "Iowa!" Most would give me a second look wondering, did I really say Iowa that state in the middle of nowhere. People whom I spoke to in other countries simply never heard of Iowa or didn't know much about it.

Iowa is one of the greatest farming states in the United States. It ranked second only to California in total value of crops and livestock. Iowa has about a fourth of the riches farmland in the United Sates.

Iowa has four distinct seasons of weather: fall, winter, spring and summer. The fall is beautiful with the changing of the leaves, occasionally Iowa experiences "Indian summer," a period after a killing freeze and shortly before winter arrives. Snow season can range from as early as mid-October to mid-April. Spring seasons are wet, and thunderstorms are annual, occurring between April and September. Summers are warm and humid and occasionally bring on the threat of severe weather such as tornados.

There are two major rivers in Iowa, the Mississippi and Missouri Rivers. The Mississippi River winds past Dubuque, Iowa. This river forms Iowa's eastern border. All rivers and streams in the state flow into the Missouri river system. As these rivers approach the Mississippi, most of the valleys are deep and limestone cliffs appear. The Des Moines River, which flows through Iowa is the largest river. It drains nearly a fourth of the state.

We walked every day across the bridge in bobby socks. 'Yah' it was so c-o-l-d! We walked about a fourth mile in rain, snow, or sleet across the bridge over-looking the Des Moines River. I would carry my violin, which I played in the Elementary Orchestra. The orchestra consisted of the 4th, 5th, and 6th grades. I continued to play the violin throughout high school. One of my fondest memories was traveling to Des Moines, Iowa for a concert and playing "G-minor symphony". I loved playing the violin at church with my sisters and Evelyn who accompanied me on the piano. Some of the most beautiful lakes dot the countryside just northwest of Fort Dodge, Iowa. The popular resort areas include Clear Lake, Okoboji, Spirit Lake, Storm Lakes and West Lakes. Our family loved to go to Lake Okoboji for picnics. Dad would drive us in his A-Model Ford we called, "rag mop". Mom would pack us a lunch of fried chicken and potato salad and we enjoyed this fun day. On the way home we would play games as pity-pat and sing songs. We loved to count the cars of various kinds and find out what state the license plates came from.

Iowa is sometimes called the Corn State, and is known as "the land where the tall corn grows". About a fifth of the nations supply of corn grows in dark fertile soil. My sisters and I use to de-tassel corn (that is pick them off the vine). This was a summer job for high school students. We were taken to one of the farms in a pick up truck. On our way to the farm, we sang songs until we arrived at our destination. When we arrived there were endless rows of corn to pick. I remember when I sat in the field to take a rest and was fired from the job. (ha-ha) I was so happy to be fired. I didn't like the job anyway.

Corn of course is Iowa's leading crop. The farmers feed much of the corn to the hogs. More hogs are raised in Iowa than in any other state. Iowa is also a leading producer of beef cattle, dairy products, oats, and soybeans. In Iowa, the most important manufacturing activity is meatpacking. Several Iowa cities have busy stockyards. Fort Dodge was the home to one of the largest meat packing plants called Tobin. Today it is known as Hormel. My sister Jeannette worked at the plant and retired there too.

I would like to share stories that shaped my childhood and tell about my beautiful, loving family, and what it was like growing up in Fort Dodge, Iowa. To start out, my father, the Rev. Leroy Patterson, was a courageous, faithful, and loving man. He always said he was a "Jack of all trades and a master of none". My father tells us about his move from Baton Rouge, Louisiana where he was born, to Fort Dodge, Iowa. This move changed his outlook on life significantly. It had been said that African American men were sent to Fort Dodge to work on the Illinois Central Railroad.

Upon arrival to Fort Dodge, he went to work for Illinois Central Railroad. I often think about how strong willed and courageous my father was to travel so far away from home and go work some place he was not familiar with. I can just imagine how overwhelming that could have been. Through dad's faith and the grace of God, he made it through.

African Americans came to Fort Dodge in the late nineteenth century to work for the Illinois Central Railroad. Most of the workers settled in "The Flats" an area of town between the rail line and the Des Moines River. Most of the African American railroad workers were originally from Louisiana like my father. History shows that the first groups of African Americans to move to Fort Dodge in 1881 were from Tennessee. They came to work in the coalmines. They spent the winter to work and later returned to Tennessee. Several families remained in Fort Dodge to live. Most of the 120 African Americans at the turn of the century were descended from these families.

The Illinois Central Railroad was also referred to as the Main Line of Mid-America. The railroad's primary routes were located in the central United States, connecting Chicago, Illinois with New Orleans and Mobile, Alabama. A line also connected Chicago with Sioux City, Iowa and another significant branch from Omaha, Nebraska, west of Fort Dodge, Iowa.

When dad came to Fort Dodge, Iowa he was part of the Great Migration. The great migration took place between 1915-1960 in which over five million southern blacks migrated to the north and west. It was one of the largest internal migrations in United States History, which forever changed the landscape of the rural south, and urban north. The first large movement occurred during World War I when over 450,000 southern blacks moved north. In the 1920's when my dad was a young man, over 800,000 blacks left the south. Dad left Louisiana for a number of reasons, to escape the oppressive economic conditions in the south for better job opportunities, and the promise of greater prosperity in the north.

World War I created a huge demand for workers in Northern factories as a result of the loss of 5 million men who left to serve in the armed forces. Prior to this the better paying jobs in factories and railroads in the north, were usually filled by European immigrants. The flood of immigrants stopped and was restricted after the war broke out. This was a result of The Immigration Act of 1924 (The

Johnson-Reed Act). This act limited the number of immigrants allowed entry into the United States. There were some areas in the north that needed workers so desperately that they actually paid African Americans to migrate north and provided free railroad passes to get them there. I can only imagine how overwhelming the transition from the south to the north was for my father. This took a lot of courage and determination. As a young man, not only did he move to a place that was unfamiliar, but also had to deal with the resentment and prejudice from the northern whites just as he did to a greater degree in the south. At this time in 1940 we were living in the most historic period in race relations in this country. In being an African American family, there is no way of denying the subject of race in Fort Dodge. As children, I can say that we didn't feel the pressure of prejudice around us, because being brought up in Christian family with love, support and prayer. Our parents, church and the Black community in Fort Dodge helped diminish the harsh experience of racism. We had a nice diverse group of friends and we had the best of both worlds.

After my father started his work for the Illinois Central Railroad and was settled in, he sent for my mother, his sweetheart, Agnes Bankston from New Orleans, LA. Shortly thereafter they were married. It should be noted that my mother was 18 years of age when she was married and my dad was 20. An addition to my mother and father migrating north to Iowa, my mom's sister, from New Orleans, Annelle

Banks joined them as well and started their family. She traveled from New Orleans to Fort Dodge, Iowa and later met and married Charles Banks. Their children were Gerolyn and Charles Banks.

The couple my dad was acquainted with during this time in Fort Dodge was a minister from Coppin Chapel A.M.E Church, the Rev. E. Johnson. Rev. Johnson married my dad, and mom and also helped them find their first home. They moved in a two level house at 1019 South First Street. Our house was across from Becker Florist gardens. I remember how they would give us flowers when picking them from the garden. My sisters and I would sit on the porch, watching people coming and going to purchase flowers from Becker's Florist. The flower gardens and the fall foliage were so beautiful to see. Mother ordered flowers frequently for our church.

Mr. and Mrs. Madison were dear friends of my parents who also helped them get settled in town. Mr. Madison was impressed with my father's compassion for being kind to people. Rev. Johnson convinced my dad to study for the ministry. During their early years of marriage dad was studying for the ministry, plus working for the Illinois Central Railroad. When dad completed his courses for ministry and Pastor Johnson was transferred to another church, our dad, the Rev. Leroy Patterson, became the pastor of Coppin Chapel AME. Evelyn was the musician for the church.

I can remember when dad lectured to couples who were getting married in our church. Whenever a person from church was ill, he would go to their home to pray for them. This was his personality and he believed strongly in helping any one whom needed his advise. My parents were so warm and welcoming. Whenever there were new couples at church visiting, my parents would invite them to our home for dinner. My sisters would be busy setting the table and getting ready for the guest.

Harry's Chicken Shack was between Illinois Central Round House and the Engineer Coal Company. It was a real treat when dad brought dinner home from Harry's Chicken Shack after work. People from all the local areas came to eat his famous chicken. Now there are many chicken franchises such as Kentucky Fried, Pop-Eyes and others.

Illinois Central Round House

The flood of 1954 prompted the city to move everyone out of the flood area and relocate our homes in other parts of the city. The Urban Renewal was put into action and completed. Many had to give up their beautiful gardens and homes. Becker Florist was one of the businesses that needed to be relocated along with our family's home. Today there is Sunkist Meadows Golf course where homes used to be. Whenever we went to Fort Dodges to visit Mom, John would take his golf clubs to play especially at our class reunion. We visited our friends Dick and Adeline Ruge, who both were my classmates. John and Dick played golf, while Adeline and I enjoyed talking about her flower garden and baking. She baked yummy breads and pastries.

Patterson's home after the 1954 flood relocation

To capture the essence of my father, I wanted to share some special memories from my nephew Mark Gates that our entire family can relate to:

Grandfather Patterson:

A very hard worker, even when retired and well into his 80s and early 90s he always had some kind of project going on. Whether it was painting the trim on the house, fixing his lawn mower or working in the garden, he kept himself busy with home projects. He was also quick to put me to work, I would come over and he would ask, "You feel like cutting some grass?" Little did I know, there were hedges and raking in store for me as well. He was very meticulous about how things were done also. After cutting the grass, not only did I have to put the lawn mover back in the basement, he wanted the lawn mower cleaned before it was put away. He was 59 years older than me and had the energy of a young man. When I was tired of mowing and trimming hedges, he was still going. Oh, and he always had to inspect my work, he was very hands on, he'd show me the correct (Leroy Patterson) way of doing things. :)

My reward for doing the work was usually a piece of orange chewy candy from his office, followed by his famous root beer made from Hires Root beer Extract. Grandfather would work on his project until past dinner and then would sit down and enjoy a cigar while watching one of his favorite spaghetti westerns, either Gun smoke or Big Valley. And when the fist fighting on TV would ensue, he would point at the TV and just crack up laughing.

For such a little man, Grandfather had a very deep voice. I remember the song we used to sing at the close of Sunday service, "Praise God from who all Blessings Flow" He's baritone voice still resonates with me.

• • •

In this life we can do no great things, just small things with Great Love.

Mother Theresa

 My mother was an extraordinary woman. She was an exceptional, mother, wife, and homemaker. She organized the house activities. She assigned us chores such as, washing dishes, hanging clothes outside on the line, cleaning floors, and helping with cooking. Mom rotated the chores between all of the sisters to make sure that when we grew up, and had our own household we would know what to do. She was training us for the future.

I loved cooking in the kitchen with mom. My favorite was baking cookies and cakes. She made the most delicious pound cake. Her famous pound cake recipe has been handed down within the family for several generations. Mom was the best cook ever. She cooked the most delicious meals. Her special Sunday dinner was fried chicken, ear corn, biscuits, and apple cobbler. So good and smelling the aroma as you walked through the house.

Dad loved rice, so mom cooked it everyday with many vegetables from her garden. It was not a meal if there was no rice. John and I brought her a rice pot from Japan and she loved it. Mom would get up early on Sunday to cook so when we come from church the dinner was prepared.

At home we always sat down at the table together to eat dinner. Each one of us would say a verse before we ate. We had conversation of what happened in school that day. We couldn't wait to get our hands on those hot biscuits. I believe my parents lived their life with hard work, enthusiasm, and energy. I inherited my mom's good spirit and personality. She lived to the age of 85 years.

Special memories about Grandmother Patterson from Mark:

Grandmother was an early riser; she would be up by 5 or 6 every morning. Whether it was house cleaning, grocery shopping or sewing, she would start early so that she could relax at 2:00 pm to watch General Hospital.

Then after the show she would call my Mom to discuss what happened. "Jeannette did you see the show today? Those people are a mess." Grandmother was an excellent cook, what made her such a good cook was that she didn't need a recipe. She could make anything. She always made Red Beans and Rice on Mondays - it's suppose to bring you good luck. For someone of her age she was rather independent. She would prepare dinner but if Grandfather was working on something, she'd call him for dinner and if he didn't come, she would go ahead and eat, but would always leave him a plate on the stove.

During the early years of marriage dad was studying for the ministry, plus working for the ICR. Together, they raised six girls and we were born two years apart. Our names from oldest to youngest: Evelyn, Cora Lee, Jeannette, myself - Gloria Delores, Beverly, and Shirley Ann. Shirley (Titi) was born nine years after Beverly. We had a brother who was the first-born. When he was one year old, he made his first step, fell and died of a heart condition. We all had different personalities as cheerful, humble, contented, talkative, enthusiastic, playful, and funny. We were a loving family who shared our lives together. I'm very proud of my sisters that have been successful in their own decisions to make things happen.

My mom was a good loving, caring person, for she took care of Emerson Manly while his grandmother worked in Lake Okoboji, a resort. We thought of him as our brother. We had lots of fun teasing him about being the only boy among the girls. He was a pleasant person and easy to get alone with. As an adult Emerson, became a very talented chef in Milwaukee, WI. We will always remember his huge homemade cinnamon rolls.

My sisters and I were born and grew up in northwest Iowa. We disagreed with one another; we played, fought, laughed and teased. I would hide under the bed when we were going to sleep and tried to scare my sisters. Did we get a spanking? Yes! Our parents disciplined us all. I was a bit mischievous sometime. Shirley, the youngest sister was always playing jokes, with pinching and pocking her tongue out and getting into a lot of trouble. We called her a spoiled brat, for she was the youngest girl. ha-ha. We would always forget and forgive. My father always preached about forgiving.

Dad had a special way of recognizing people who were kind and generous to the family. He would always send thank-you notes. I remember when John and I would go home to visit. Dad would always send a thank-you note saying,

I want to thank-you and John for visiting us. We enjoyed your visit.

Leroy Patterson

I inherited my dad's courage and determination.

My mom also would send lovely notes on very pretty stationary. I inherited my mom's personality and artistic ability.

Dad used to say in his sermon, "Ye shall know the truth and the truth shall make you free" and this Bible verse is one of my favorites. You can't know the truth until you are willing to know yourself. Another one of my dad's favorite quotes was by Frederick Douglass:

> *It is not fair play to start the Negro out in life, from nothing and with nothing, while others start with the advantage of a thousand years behind them. He should be measured, not by the heights others have obtained, but from the depths from which he has come.*

We all went to Riverside Elementary School. All my sisters walked to school every day. When we didn't take our lunch, we walked home, and Mom would have either beans and rice, or spaghetti and meatballs. "Wow" it was so good.

Elementary School, Junior High and Senior High School were close enough from our house for us to walk. Our activities were centered around the YWCA, skating parties, and Girl Scouts and church activities. Sunday school played an important part in our lives. We got up and dressed for Sunday school and stayed for church. Since every store was closed on Sundays, we entertained each other with music. Evelyn played the piano at home and we could sing as she accompanied us. One of the songs she would play was "Lean

On Me". We would harmonize it with Jeannette and Cora as soprano; Beverly and I sang alto, and this we sure did enjoy. Sometimes we would add instruments. Cora would play her guitar and I played the violin. This was the entertainment we did at home when we were not teasing one another.

The Six Joys

Let love and faithfulness never leave you; bind them around your neck, write them on the tablet of your heart.

Proverbs 3:3

Top row (l-r) **Evelyn, Jeanette, Cora Lee**
Bottom row (l-r) **Gloria, Beverly, Shirley**

Since there are six girls in our family I research about first-born, middle child, or last-born. If the same parents raise brothers and sisters, then how do they end up so different? One sibling grows up to be successful academically, with few friends, while another becomes the athlete with loads of friends. To the degree that one of the siblings is a responsible person, another will be attention seeking or rebellious. There are always exceptions. For example, if the first two children are born close together, and the third child comes along much later, the last-born may have characteristics resembling the first child.

Here are some characteristics:

Only children are usually mature for their age, are perfectionists, leaders and conscientious. They often get along better with people older than themselves. Only children love to be alone. This is the result of their place in the family. Only children tend to be organizers, schedulers and worriers. They are normally fair, dependable and have been known to throw tantrums to show power. The only child has a tendency to have a sarcastic sense of humor.

First-born children have some similar characteristics between the first-born and the only child. All first-born children were at one time the only child. Suddenly, another child has entered the family and the first-born must find another way to establish their place in the family. Common personalities of the first-born include perfectionism, controlling, reliable, conscientiousness, organized, list maker, and goal oriented. First-born children tend to be considered more advanced or "little adults." They can develop into two basic personality types, compliant and pleasant or strong-willed and aggressive. First-born children commonly go on in life to be leaders and achievers. Over half of the U.S. presidents were first-born.

Second-born children must cope with the oldest child taking away attention by outperforming him or her. They have the challenge of overcoming the authority of the first-born by being a perfectionist. The second-born feels that no one cares about how they feel, because the oldest child clearly does not. They often feel 'not good enough' or inadequate to parents and strive to please them. They are detailed, thorough and disciplined. They like everything to be in balance. First-born children are often the diplomats of the family preferring peace and feels overwhelmed when others are angry.

Middle children are often opposite of their older sibling. Middle children often feel like their older brother/sister gets all the glory while the youngest escapes all discipline. They can usually read people well, for they are peacemakers who see all sides of a situation, and are independent and inventive. They can also be somewhat rebellious.

Fourth-born children are thoughtful, intuitive, social, outgoing, and creative. They tend to be expressive and loving, responding to any family members sadness or pain. The fourth born wants everyone to get along and is happy when the family is happy.

Gap children that are five or more years apart tend to adapt first-born traits. The greater the age distance between siblings, the less the siblings will affect each other.

Last born children are described as sociable, charming, loving, and open, but also temperamental and out going. They are accused of being spoiled, the one who gets everything the other sibling never had. The last one gets an abundance of attention and often is the target of jokes.

Evelyn Patterson Russell – Compassionate

Evelyn is the first-born child in our family. As a teenage girl she was interested in playing the piano. She took piano lessons from a neighbor who was a teacher and taught Evelyn how to play. She was a very good teacher. Evelyn loved to play the piano and became a very good musician. She was the musician for Coppin Chapel in Fort Dodge. She was a wife, musician, and godmother of Robert Franklin. Being the oldest sister she cared for the youngest sisters whenever our parents attended church events. After graduating from Fort Dodge High she visited and moved to St Paul, MN. She was employed at the United States Ammunition Factory during World War II and later gained employment with the Minnesota Department of Human Rights. She worked as a receptionist/secretary. While there she was the recipient of an award from Governor Perpich after 31 years of service for her faithful commitment. Governor Perpich proclaimed Tuesday, June 16, 1987 to be Evelyn Russell Day. Evelyn was an active member of St. James A.M.E Church in Saint Paul, MN. She was involved with the Cherub Youth Choir serving the church as pianist/organist. She was an accomplish pianist and enjoyed performing for various occasions. Evelyn had a loving and compassionate personality. Evelyn and her husband Carl Russell loved to travel and visit family and friends. Her deep values were instilled in her by our parents Rev. Leroy and Agnes Patterson. Evelyn went to finish her work in heaven (1-1-11). This was a day to remember.

Cora Lee Patterson– Charming

 Cora was the second of six girls. She was a wife, homemaker, and receptionist. She graduated from Business College in Fort Dodge. Cora worked at Younkers department store, one of the largest in Fort Dodge. She married and lived in Chicago. After a while she came back to her roots in Fort Dodge. She preferred the country rather than the city. She was an active member of Coppin Chapel A.M.E. Church, where she was

church secretary and helped Dad with typing out his sermons. Cora enjoyed playing the guitar. She was always seen with a smile on her face and possessed a kind and thoughtful personality.

Jeannette Patterson Gates - Caring

Jeannette was the third in line. She was a wife, mother, grandma, and great-grandma. She had a very tranquil nature and had a great sense of humor. She got along with all of her sisters. She was the peacemaker. Jeanette was so creative. Mother taught her how to embroidery and crochet and with her creativity she made beautiful placemats for the dinner table. Jeanette eventually moved to Minnesota, where her son and daughter lived.

Jeanette fondest life memories of Ford Dodge, in her own words:

I'm the quiet one of the bunch, but I've also been known to have a great sense of humor. A year after graduating from Fort Dodge Senior High, I started working at Tobin Meatpacking plant, which later became Hormel. I remember that period of time as being fun for me; I was making a good living. My friends were Leona Howard and my sister Cora Lee. This was the time of the big band sound like Count Basie and his orchestra, Duke Ellington, and lots of dances at the YWCA and the Royal 400, where Cora Lee used to tap dance.

It was at one of the YWCA sponsored dances that I met and later married Walter Gates in 1953. Together we have four children – Walter Lynn is the oldest and lives in St. Paul with his wife and two children; Pam, now living in Des Moines, has five children; Mark lives in Minneapolis, and Annette also lives in Minneapolis. I have seven grandchildren and four great-grandchildren. Although Walter and I divorced some years ago, we still remain close friends.

I am so very proud of my family. They have all been successful in their own way and continue to be great kids. About eight years ago I moved to the Twin Cities to be near my sisters Gloria, Evelyn, and Shirley as well as my children. Unfortunately, we lost Cora Lee a year before I moved to Minneapolis. Not only was she my beloved sister, she was one of my closest and dearest friends. She was and continues to be our "angel". I am so fortunate to have had Leroy and Agnes Patterson as parents and to have such loving sisters. I am definitely a blessed woman with no regrets.

These days I live in a very nice senior living facility where I enjoy my exercise classes, making crafts greeting cards and listening to my favorite recording artist, Sarah Vaughn. I also enjoy spending time with my children and adore my canine grandson, Charlie who belongs to my son Mark.

Although I don't get back to Fort Dodge that often, I have such fond memories of the place I still consider home.

Gloria Delores Hazelwood – Creative

I'm the fourth and middle child. The middle child often feels left out because the oldest and youngest set all the attention. I'm not the oldest; I'm not the youngest. My birth month is October and my gemstones (opal), it is regarded as good luck and blessed with a business, Mary Kay. The opal also pertains to love meaning that I had a high chance of finding my true love, and I definitely found it. You will read more about me later.

Beverly DeJohnette – Confident

Beverly is the fifth sister. She is a wonderful mom. She is energetic and loves adventure. She would always help mom comb and style our hair before leaving for church. She made her home in Los Angeles, California. Beverly became very successful as a hair stylist in Los Angeles. She loved to read educational books and work on her computer to research all kinds of subjects. One of her hobbies is cooking. Her favorite type of food to cook is various Chinese cuisines. Sometimes Beverly bakes cakes for her son Gilbert. On weekends she enjoys shopping and going to restaurants in Beverly Hills, California.

Beverly shares a brief summary of her life in Fort, Dodge and Los Angeles, CA. in her own words

My birth name is Beverly Ann Patterson, and I am the fifth sister born. I grew up in Fort Dodge, Iowa, and after graduating from high school I moved to Des Moines, Iowa to pursue a career in cosmetology. Two years later, I moved to Chicago, Illinois where I got married, and my husband and I moved to Los Angeles, California where my son Gilbert Lewis was born. He grew up in Los Angeles and finished college with a major in mathematics. My life growing up with my family has left a lot of happy memories.

Shirley Ann Williams (Titileyo)— Energetic

Shirley is the sixth in line and the youngest in the family. She is vivacious and a fun loving sister. After high school she attended Wilberforce University in Zenia,

Ohio. She is an educator who teaches children and adults. She loves to read, do water aerobics, dance and yoga. Most of all traveling abroad has been her favorite, to see and experience how other cultures live. Some of the places she has visited are West Africa (Ghana, Ivory Coast), Southern Africa (Namibia, South Africa), and Paris, France. Shirley is a United States family host for international students. She has hosted students from China, Japan, Venezuela, Dominican Republic and Brazil.

When Shirley relaxes she likes to cook and try different kinds of foods. Her secret recipe of mmm - fried chicken and you don't have to watch your calories. Shirley is a dedicated mother, teacher, grandma and loves the company of family and friends.

She has three children, Eric Demitrius, Stokley Mandela and Kamali Missale. Eric is a professional painter, Kamali is director of Marketing & Strategic Partnerships in New York and Stokley is the lead singer of a band called Mint Condition. Stokley has a wife, Sylvia and two children, Aaliyah and Arion. I'm very proud of my sisters that have been successful in their own decisions to make things happen.

In this life we can do no great things, just small things with great love.

Mother Theresa

The Beauty of a Woman

The beauty of a woman is not in the clothes she wears, the figure she carries, or the way she combs her hair.

The beauty of a woman must be seen from in her eyes, because that is the doorway to her heart, the place where love resides.

The beauty of a woman is not in a facial mole, but true beauty in a woman is reflected in her soul.

It is caring that she lovingly gives the passion that she shows, and the beauty of a woman with passing years only grows!

Gloria D. Hazelwood

"I love those who love me; and those who diligently seek me will find me."

Proverbs 8:17

I am the 4th girl of six in our family. I remember I would carry my violin, which I played in the orchestra in elementary school. The orchestra consisted of the 4th, 5th, and 6th grades. In high school I continued to play the violin. Our orchestra practiced playing "G-Minor Symphony", and we traveled to Des Moines, Iowa for a concert. I loved playing the violin at church with my sister Evelyn, who accompanied me by playing the piano. I also took piano lessons with my sister. I just loved music. I loved swimming because in our physical education classes at Fort Dodge High School, we were taught to swim. We were required to dive and swim across the pool before graduating. Our teacher, Ms. Nordstrom believed that teaching swimming helps to save our lives and others. I had a fear of deep water however, when it was my turn to dive in the pool I said a little prayer and dove in. I overcame my fear and swam the whole lap. This showed me that even though one has fear, it doesn't have to stop you from accomplishing things. Swim aerobics has become one of my favorite activities. I have been going to Lifetime Fitness aerobics class three times a week. This is great exercise. It makes me feel so invigorated and energized.

Different times in my journey I was able to create interest in everything I've done. Anything can be a blessing, miracle, or opportunity to choose to do what you want. In being creative, I must mention this about me that most people don't know. I really enjoy playing the piano and genie organ. The genie is smaller than regular organ. It has magical features with the ability to do many musical instruments; for instance you can make it sound like a guitar, banjo, flute, or trumpet. It could sound like any instrument you could imagine. It was very entertaining. I took lessons and learned simple songs like "What a Wonderful World," "The Entertainer," and other songs for my enjoyment. John and I had fun playing song together. Growing up I was the only one who liked to listen to symphony music. My sisters would put cotton in their ears when I practiced my violin. "Yeah" that is true.

When I was very young, I would spend my leisure time sketching faces and making doll clothes. I always said that I wanted to be a fashion designer when I grew up. After graduating from Fort Dodge High School, I enrolled in Central State College in Oberlin, Ohio. The reason I enrolled in this particular College is that my father at this time was the pastor of Coppin Chapel A.M.E Church and the church had given scholarships to students. I was so excited about this venture. Mom helped me to pack my trunk for college. This trunk was just like a cedar chest. I joined the sorority Alpha Kappa Alpha (AKA). I also took my violin to play in various musicals. I really enjoyed the college life.

My first year of college, I met many friends. I had two very friendly roommates, Nancy and Barbara. My roommate Barbara went to school for a "Mrs. Degree". Her plan was to find a husband and get married. She even barrowed my clothes for her dates. Barbara was married by the end of freshman year. I remember my mom sending me care packages and everyone wondering what was in the box. My mom would always send me her delicious cookies. I would always share them with my classmates. I also designed and made my clothes and shared them with my roommates. I considered fashion design school in Cleveland, Ohio, because of my self-taught fashion design skills. The Madisons who were friends of my parents lived in Cleveland. They were originally from Fort Dodge, but moved to Ohio. When I enrolled in Elizabeth Kardos Fashion Institute I lived with the Madisons and I was very eager and delighted to learn about designing clothes. I studied pattern drafting. This was the beginning of how clothes were made, piece-by-piece. I learned how to sketch, design, make patterns, finish garments, and model clothes for customers. Yes, this was really fantastic! I loved what I was doing, and my dream came true – I completed design school. Hurrah!

I was looking for a fabulous job in the fashion business. I wanted to design and draft garments. This would involve traveling to find that kind of job. I was very excited about what I wanted to do to complete my dream in working in the fashion designing business. I had planned to be successful in the designing field, but the love bug interfered. This is what the Lord had planned for my life. I thought of what I wanted in my life, working in a studio in New York, drafting and designing clothes, traveling, or teaching. These things came to my mind, and life is what you make it, so enjoy it whatever you do. I believed that the Lord was directing my steps.

During this time, I had been corresponding with my college sweetheart, John E. Hazelwood who was, handsome, and kindhearted man. I met him while I was at Central State College. John was from Cambridge, Ohio. He had just graduated from Wilberforce University with a degree in chemistry and math and was interested in working in the medical field. His college was across from Central State. John became a second lieutenant in the Reserve Officer Training Corps (ROTC) and completed the training course and had orders to go to Korea. Upon my love leaving, he asked me to marry him. WOW! I had plans to go in the fashion business as a career woman, and John was leaving for Korea. However, John convinced me that I could continue my career, while he was away. My intuition said YES, why not!

John had such a warm-hearted family. He had two sisters and a brother. His sisters' names were Ruth and Harriet. His brother was Jim Hazelwood. His father, Bufford, raised the family on a farm in Cambridge, Ohio. John's mother died when he was three years old. John was the youngest in his family. His family encouraged and supported John to be successful in his career.

In 1954, we had initially planned our wedding to be in the fall, however John received military orders to leave for Korea by July. We had only one month to plan our wedding before he left to go to Korea. Our wedding was held in Cleveland, Ohio. I bought my wedding dress with the help of the Madison family.

I designed my reception dress. It was green taffeta with matching shoes. My designer training paid off. It was stunning! John's uncle, Doc Hazelwood, played an unusually beautiful song for us on the piano. He was a music professor. His family in Cambridge, Ohio planned the wedding dinner.

My family was unable to come to Cleveland to see us marry, so they prepared for our reception in Iowa. We traveled by train to Iowa on our honeymoon, which was very exciting. As we traveled we talked about our future plans for when he came back from Korea. I was thinking about staying with my parents at this time while he was away. It was a very scenic trip going west. We finally arrived in Fort

Wedding Reception
(l-r) Gloria, John, Jeanette, Leroy, Shirley, Charles,
Gerolyn, Evelyn, Beverly, Agnes, Cora Lee, Annell

Wedding Reception
Top row (l-r) Beverly, Shirley
Bottom row (l-r) Jeanette, Evelyn, John, Gloria, Cora Lee,
Leroy, Agnes

My reception dress. It was green taffeta with matching shoes

My Wedding Dress

Dodge, Iowa. John was delighted to meet my family. He loved my mom. My family was excited to meet John and was happy with my decision to marry. John asked my father, "Do all these girls gang up on you?" Dad would laugh and say, "No, they are very good girls." The family just loved him. John left for Korea, and I decided to stay in Iowa with my family. I got a job working at Younkers Department Store in Fort Dodge, working in the drapery department. It was a very interesting job measuring and cutting material for windows. I learned how to make valances for my future home. My sister Cora Lee also worked at Younkers in another department.

The Flood of 1954

U. S. Geological Survey, Water Resources Division 1959

The flood of June 1954

The Flats was the area between the Illinois Central Railroad tracks and the Des Moines River extending from Central Avenue to the Coleman District. There were two bridges spanning the Flats – Herring and Bennett viaducts, three railroads, and many, many businesses that serviced the Flats area.

Reverend and Mrs. Leroy Patterson lived at 1019 South 1st Street Flats. See map on the next page.

Excerpted from Memorable Days of the Flats: Fort Dodge, Iowa by Harold Hill

The flood of June 1954 was caused by exceptionally heavy rainfall. The center of the heavy June rains was near the eastern boundary of the basin with eight-day totals exceeding 12 inches. All of the basins above Fort Dodge received rainfall in excess of six inches. Record peak discharges occurred on the East Fork and on the main stem downstream as far as Des Moines. This caused the Des Moines River to crest at 19 feet, 4 inches. Flooding occurs at 10 feet, 6 inches.

Floods in the upper Des Moines River Basin, Iowa by Harlan H. Schwob, Hydraulic Engineer, United States Geological Survey 1970.

As a result of the flood the city moved everyone (homes and businesses) out of the flood area and relocated everyone into homes in other parts of the city.

The Flats

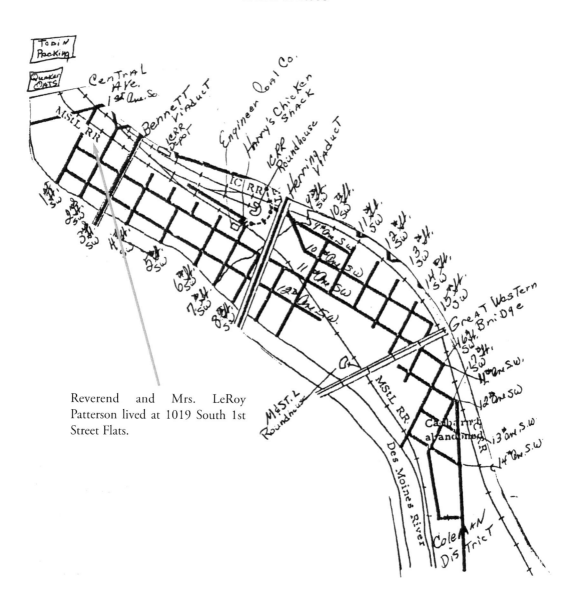

Reverend and Mrs. LeRoy Patterson lived at 1019 South 1st Street Flats.

1954 Supreme Court Decision on Brown v. Board of Education of Topeka, Kansas

On May 17, 1954, U.S. Supreme Court Justice Earl Warren delivered the unanimous ruling in the landmark civil rights case Brown v. Board of Education of Topeka, Kansas. State-sanctioned segregation of public schools was a violation of the 14th amendment and was, therefore, unconstitutional. This historic decision marked the end of the "separate but equal" precedent set by the Supreme Court nearly 60 years earlier in Plessy v. Ferguson and served as a catalyst for the expanding civil rights movement during the decade of the 1950s.

After John returned from Korea, he had orders to go to Fort Benning, Georgia. We drove to Georgia; it was our first trip traveling south, and it was different. This was my first time being exposed to prejudice.

To frame what was happening during that time, our country was filled with hatred and racism. One example of this was the " Little Rock Nine". These were nine black children who had to be protected by the National Guard so they could attend an all white high school in Arkansas. President Eisenhower, our nations president at the time, sent the 101st Airborne Division to little Rock to protect the students. The white mob was very angry about black kids entering there school and did everything they could to stop it. Some of the black children were spit on; beat and one child even had acid thrown in their eyes.

We never experienced racism to that degree but it still sickened me to see hatred and bigotry that surrounded us throughout the south. For the first time in my life I saw the separation of the races. There were signs for whites and blacks only. Whites had their own water fountains, restrooms, restaurants, and movie theaters. Blacks were designated to certain areas. When traveling on a bus, blacks had to sit in the back or stand. From growing up in Fort Dodge, Iowa, this outright discrimination was hard for me to understand.

I remember when I went shopping for clothes with one of my friends. As we entered into the store the sales lady asked us to leave. She stated in an abrupt tone that she could not sell me anything. We left and went next door to a shoe store. They asked us to go to the back of the store. I refused. I asked, "Why?" I wanted those shoes and I refused to go to the back of that store. I stood my ground. As I stood out in front of the store, the storeowner hesitantly allowed me to stay in front of the store and I purchased the shoes and left. I could not believe the ignorance of someone treating another human being with such disrespect, because his or her skin was a different color.

The military base was quite interesting. There were rambler style homes with beautiful thick green grass. We loved our new home on the military base. What made it even better is that we had great neighbors. We met some terrific people like our good friends Roscoe and Milly Robinson, Carl and Nellie Burhanan, and Alvin and Faye Arnold. Some of our other acquaintances were William and Billy Walker, and Jim and Janie Marshall. We all had big dreams and high expectations and were destined for success. One example, Roscoe Robinson Jr. retired at the honorable rank of a Four Star General and this was quite an accomplishment. We all were young military families just beginning our new lives. We still keep in touch by cards, e-mail, or phone. The weather in Georgia was lovely. That is one thing I liked about the state. We did not have cloths dryer like today. I had an outside clothesline to hang my sheets out on the line. I loved the smell of fresh laundered cloths hanging outside to dry. We were in Fort Benning for three years. In 1957, at the end of the assignment John Jr. was born. John Jr. and I flew to Fort Campbell, Kentucky for the next assignment. Kentucky had very good temperatures and weather. I really enjoyed the people and shopping.

First Home in Fort Benning, Georgia

In 1958 our daughter, Brenda Lee, was born. John Jr. and Brenda were sixteen months apart. John was a paratrooper in the 101st Airborne Division at Fort Campbell. The children and I would go watch him jump out of the planes and then parachute down to the ground. There were demonstrations and air shows that were quite exhilarating. I would always pray that John was safe landing.

At the end of the three years, John had his next assignment to Mainz-Goshenhein, Germany. I was excited

On a ship to Germany
(John Jr. & Brenda

to share the news with my parents about going to Europe. John flew to Germany, and the children and I traveled to Fort Dix, New Jersey en route to Germany. Other dependents were taking the same trip to Germany. We boarded the ship, and I felt a bit apprehensive about traveling to Germany with two young children that were two and three years old.

My children did very well on the ship; running, jumping, laughing, and they loved looking out the window with the waves. Halfway through the trip there was this turbulent, rough weather across the ocean. I became ill on the trip while John Jr. and Brenda were still having fun with the up-and-down bumps from the sea. Finally, we arrived in Mainz, Germany after three days of travel. I will not travel by ship again on such a long trip.

Mainz is situated on the Rhine River. It has been a busy trading center since Roman times. It is the capital of the state of Phineland-Palatinate and a University City in Germany. John met us at the port. Oh, what gorgeous scenery in Germany! This trip was a challenge for me, and I was given lots of wisdom from my experience on this long journey with John Jr. and Brenda.

At this time we didn't have government quarters, so John had approval to move the family in a German housing complex near the base. Our landlords were Frau and Weir Heinrich, a German couple. Frau and Weir did not speak English, and we did not speak German. This dilemma made it perfect for both families to learn each other's language. John wasn't home often because of his military commitments so our time was spent with the Heinrichs.

Since we could not speak the language, I thought of ways we could communicate. I would point to different objects as the table. Frau would answer me in German, and I was beginning to add words to my vocabulary by pointing and listening. Some words I learned were brat (bread), fleisch (beef), and boden (floor). This was an excellent way to learn German. The Heinrich's treated us as part of their family. They took us to the meat market for shopping. Weir would say "Wir gingen einkaufen in der Fleischerer." I would say, "We are going to shop for some meat." She would say, "Wir waren einkaufen

John, Frau & Weir, Mainz-Goshenhein, Germany

in der Backerei." I would say, "We are going to the bakery." It was quite interesting to see how they prepared for their afternoon tea. Everyday at 2:00 p.m. we had tea and goodies. Every afternoon it was The Heinrich's tradition to set the table with beautiful china and all kinds of German cookies and delicious pastries. I now have my own teatime in the afternoon at 2:00 p.m.

Frau Heinrich enrolled John and Brenda in the German Kindar-School (kindergarten). They began to speak German very well, and I learned quite a bit with Frau. This is the best way to learn foreign languages. The teachers disciplined the class very well, and children certainly loved school. We walked to school every day to take them and bring them home. After a year living in the German neighborhood, we moved in American government quarters. All of us were very sad about leaving the Heinrich family. They had no children

John Jr. & Brenda
in Kindar School

John and Brenda in Mainz,
Germany

and had gotten so attached to John Jr. and Brenda. They came to visit us often in our new home. I had a "putzfraw" or "maid" to help me with household chores. The maid could speak a little English and we were able to communicate with one another.

While in Germany, there were many activities in which to participate. I remember learning how to play golf and joining a golf team. I joined the Officers' Wives Club, and we traveled on tours throughout Europe on vacations. We saw East and West Berlin and saw how the two cities were very different. Berlin is the largest city in Germany. When we were there, the Berlin wall separated East and West Berlin. The wall was a physical division between the two cities from 1961 to 1989. The wall represented a symbolic boundary between communism and democracy during the cold war. The wall stood strong for 28 years keeping the East Germans from fleeing to the West. When we toured the city there were restrictions, and we were not allowed to take any photos. The city in Berlin was rather dark and depressing. There was very little lighting and the buildings were old and worn. We were not allowed to get out of our tour bus. This was an interesting tour to see how the people lived, for they showed their sadness through their facial expressions. The Berlin Wall was torn down in 1989. Another interesting city in Germany was Wiesbaden. Wiesbaden was where the military airbase was located, and we loved to go shopping there for food and housewares on the weekends. Frankfurt,

Germany was another city where we visited. Frankfurt reminded me of New York City because of its impressive skyline. Frankfurt is Germany's financial and business center.

I taught cake decorating and sewing classes to women at the Officer's Wives Club. The reason I volunteered to teach the class was because it created an interest among the women, and it kept them busy in activities while their husbands were gone on military training. One of my favorite places that John and I traveled was to a ski resort in Garmish, Germany. This is where I learned how to downhill ski. The weather was so pleasant. All we need was a light sweater. I remember practicing on the easy hill when I saw John and yelled to him to watch me as I skied downhill. As soon as I turned my head back and didn't look where I was going, I almost ran into a tree. Luckily, I did not get hurt that day. Skiing in Germany was a whole lot of fun. Something I will always remember.

Gloria, John Jr. & Brenda Skiing in Germany

John and I also went to Paris, France on a vacation. We ate, slept, and shopped in Paris. The Eiffel Tower was so remarkable, with the beautiful cathedrals. We ate at one of the bistros, which were crowded day and night. The Moulin

Rouge was the most famous place for a night show of entertainment. It was absolutely marvelous. We took the family to Amsterdam, Holland. We drove from Mainz, Germany to Amsterdam. We saw the beautiful tulips and also other different colors of flowers that were very beautiful. We saw Madera Dam, which was a colorful sight to see. In Mainz,

John and the children in Amsterdam, Netherlands

Germany John and I loved to play golf. I took golf lessons and joined the Officers Women's Golf Association. We would tee off at 8 AM bright and early. I enjoyed playing with other clubs. Overall, our tour of Europe was very exciting and educational. I learned so much about the people, the culture, and the language. Our children also benefited by the experience of living in Europe.

In 1963 after living in Germany for three years, President John F. Kennedy was assassinated in Dallas Texas. The news shocked the nation. Men and women cried openly sadden from the news. It was a very mournful time for the people in the United States. The reaction in Germany was very similar, they were very sorrowful. While this was happening, we were in flight from Germany to Fort Dix, New Jersey, John's next assignment. Since the JFK's assassination in 1963, the United Stated has gone through an enormous social and political transformation. Unfortunately our county had also suffered several other senseless assassinations of other people who have had a positive impact on our country such as Dr. Martin Luther King Jr.

We stayed in Fort Dix for three years. I enrolled at the University of New Jersey to study elementary education. I had been thinking of my volunteer time teaching classes like cake decorating and sewing to the Officers' Wives Club in Germany and how teaching would be an exciting and rewarding career for me. I finished one year of college, and John was promoted to Major. His next assignment was Leavenworth, Kansas. I enrolled at the University of Kansas and completed one year of teaching courses. I had aspirations of being a teacher. I wanted students to be active learners and be interested to learn. While John was in Command and Staff College I was going to college studying. I had quite a job keeping up with the household, staying organized and keeping the children happy. I found activities for them after school to keep them busy for they had many friends.

When John finished his college program, he was reassigned to Korea. While John was in Korea, I stayed in the United States and moved to St. Paul, Minnesota. I had two sisters that lived in St. Paul. Evelyn and Shirley Ann were very happy for me to come, and they helped me find an apartment. I enrolled John Jr. and Brenda in St. Peter Claver Elementary. This was a Catholic school in the city of St. Paul. They wore uniforms to school everyday. I loved those uniforms because I didn't have to go shopping for school clothes. This was great! St. Peter Claver created good spiritual understanding for them. I went to Concordia College in St. Paul to continue my studies in education. I enjoyed my sisters helping with activities for the children on the weekends when I was studying for an exam. I always kept in my mind the goal of becoming an elementary school teacher, so that I could plan for the future of my family. The couple that we rented the apartment from in Saint Paul, had no children, yet they were very kind to my kids and treated them as if they were there own. It was great to have family close to me. Shirley and Evelyn lived only one block from me.

Hurrah!!! It was time for John to come home from Korea. Now he had an exciting assignment in Washington, D.C. to work at the Pentagon. I was very pleased about this one. We purchased our first home in Falls Church, Virginia. It was 101 Popular Drive, sitting on a little hill in a cul-de-sac. The children fell in love with the house because in the backyard there was a small playhouse. They took their toys, chairs, and friends to play in this playhouse. After a year in Washington, John had an assignment in Vietnam. I stayed in Virginia with the children so they could continue at their schools. I enrolled in D.C. Teachers College now (University

Home on 101 Poplar Drive with a playhouse in the back in
Falls Church, Virginia

of District of Columbia) in Washington, D.C. It was a 30-minute drive from Virginia and my classes were in the morning so I could get the kids from school. Living in Virginia while John was in Vietnam was a challenging time. Again I was the mom and dad the time John was gone.

We lived in Virginia for three years. We were the only black family in our neighborhood in Falls Church, Va. John Jr. and Brenda were the only black children at their elementary school. Brenda unfortunately had a hard time with her classmates while at school. They said terrible things to her like "Hey n-----!, why don't you go back to Africa where you came from" and they threatened to beat her up after school. We all got through our bad times. As Dr. Schuller says, "Tough times never last, but tough people do."

As Martin Luther King said, "The time is always right--to do what is right."

Yeah! I did it! What a great feeling that I graduated and received a Bachelor of Science degree in Education and a minor in Art Design from the District of Columbia Teachers College (University of the District of Columbia). I wanted to be a teacher and to inspire my students to be more than they thought they could. I attended four colleges  while traveling, and with persistence and tenacity I had completed my degree. I had many obstacles in my way, as transferring from one college to another because of John's numerous military assignments and raising the kids in his absence. I have been asked about the many times we have moved, and I think because I was young and ambitious and loved adventure, I handled all the moving with grace and positivity.

I applied for my first teaching job! I felt so excited about this venture. I taught the third grade in Markham Elementary in Virginia, which was a short distance from our home. On my blackboard, I wrote the Golden Rule, "Do unto others as you would have them do unto you." I was eager to connect with students who were curious about learning. A student is a better student if he or she can master their reading and math skills. My mission was to prepare these students to make a difference in the world. I kept the class in order with lots of extra work for those who needed it.

There was a great deal of turmoil about civil rights in the United States while John was at war in Vietnam. There was a lot of racial tension and hatred at this time. Within this three-year period, John was assigned to Vietnam. John was there from 1972-73. He was only suppose to be there for 12 months, but his time was extended for 16 months. This was a difficult time for

John returns home from Vietnam with Brenda and John Jr.

me to have my husband away at war. I had several friends, who were military wives, whose husbands did not return home from the war.

The United States was at war with Vietnam for a number of years. This war was one of the longest wars in American history. It finally ended in 1975. Communication was so different at this time, compared to the technology of today. The family communicated with John while he was in Vietnam by cassette tape recordings. We would sit at the dinner table and record what was happening at home and school, then send the tape off by mail. About three weeks later John would send a response back. It was always exciting to get mail from him and hear his voice.

After John's assignment in Vietnam, we left Virginia for Fort Riley, Kansas. His assignment at this time was to attend the Commander & General Staff College for the year. We moved in government quarters on the base. This house was overwhelming! "Oh, my!" This was the largest three-story home I have ever seen. We had two living rooms, a spacious

Sparky

kitchen, a large-screen porch, where our dog "Sparky," a cocker spaniel stayed. He would always bark at the garbage truck and mailman. One day he bit our dry cleaning man when he delivered our clothes. Sparky was a very good dog, however he was sometimes temperamental and didn't like strangers. When we moved to another military post we shipped Sparky by plane. He was in a crate and was happy to get out of it at the end of the trip.

I taught in Junction City Elementary School (3rd grade) in Junction City, Kansas. John was promoted to Colonel, which was his ultimate goal and became Deputy Chief of Staff. We stayed in Fort Riley for two years, and then moved back to the state of Virginia, where John was assigned to the Office Inspector General at the Pentagon. We purchased our second home in Alexandria. This time, I taught the 4th grade at Franconia Elementary School. Billy Walker and I were the only African American teachers in the school. John Jr. and Brenda Lee attended Hayfield Secondary High

School. John Jr. played football and did gymnastics and Brenda was captain of the cheerleading squad. John worked at the Pentagon for five years, plus two more years as Post Inspector General at Fort Belvoir, Virginia. This was the longest time we spent in one area.

Fort Riley Elementary School, 4th Grade

Home in Fort Riley, Kansas with Gloria, John Jr., Brenda and
Sparky

Our second home in Alexandria, Virginia

Retirement

After more than 20 years in the military John was contemplating retiring. We were ambivalent about where we wanted to live. We loved the Virginia area because we had many friends. We considered Ohio because John had family there, and Iowa because my parents lived there. We considered Minnesota because John loved the location, and my sisters Evelyn and Shirley lived there, plus my parents lived a short distance from Minnesota. Our decision was Minnesota, and we thought it was a good decision. We contacted several agencies in Minnesota to inquire about homes. John suggested that I take a trip to Minnesota to look for homes. The realtor met me at the airport and gave me a tour throughout the metro area. I told my sister that we were really undecided about St. Paul at this time. John and I made a second trip to Minnesota, and we met with a homebuilder. We worked out a plan to design and build our home. There was a piece of land located in Bloomington, and the location was perfect. We went with the plans for a Spanish-style house with black iron gates. We had a whirlpool and sky lights in the atrium, which was the focus point of the home. I enjoyed coming from school and relaxing in the whirlpool. Our garage was built to accommodate our Winnebago recreational vehicle (RV).

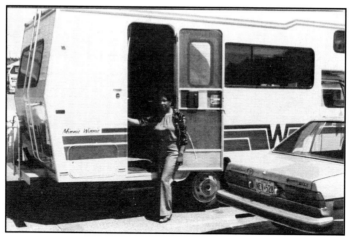

Winnebago RV

We moved to a hotel in Minneapolis while waiting for our home to be completed. We were driving our RV and had our dog Sparky with us. Our RV was used for transporting John Jr. to and from college. We enjoyed taking long vacations throughout the United States, including Alaska and Canada. We also enjoyed packing up some weekends to go north to Breezy Point and other recreational areas. Our address to our new home was 8010 Tierneys Woods Road. There were very few homes in this area, but it eventually filled up. We loved our new home. John rode the lawn mover to cut the grass, and I planted flowers around the house. John and Brenda were in college at this time. We had wonderful neighbors. After John retired from the military life he applied for an administrative position for the MN Department of Transportation (MNDOT) in Golden Valley. He was the business manager for District 5.

Our Spanish style house in Bloomington, MN

Relaxing in the whirlpool after a day at school.

During this time John Jr. and Brenda went to Bowling Green State University in Ohio. John Jr. graduated with a major in liberal arts studies. He also was commissioned as a Second Lieutenant in the US Air Force. In 1980, John married his college sweetheart, Patricia Penn, who was from Cincinnati, Ohio. She was also a graduate of Bowling Green University majoring in speech therapy.

Brenda majored in biology and minored in chemistry. She married her college sweetheart, Jackie Franklin. He graduated from Metropolitan State University and majored in business. Jackie and Brenda settled in Bloomington. Of course, Brenda wanted to be near her parents, and we felt very lucky and happy to have them here.

My children, grandchildren, and great grandchildren are the joys of my life. They give me the gift of love, just as my mom did throughout her life. She left us a tremendous gift of love and an enormous legacy of joy. My mother is our guardian angel guiding each step we take forward.

A Child's Growth

Voice says, "Because I love you best."

Real Mothers know that a child's growth is not measured by height or years or grade......

It is marked by the progression of Mommy to Mom to Mother......

4 Years of age	My Mommy can do anything!
8 Years of age	My Mom knows a lot! A whole lot!
12 Years of age	My Mother doesn't know everything!
14 Years of age	My Mother! She wouldn't have a clue.
16 Years of age	Mother? She's so five minutes ago.
18 Years of age	That old woman? She's way out of date!
25 Years of age	Well, she might know a little bit about it?
35 Years of age	Before we decide, let's get mom's opinion.
45 Years of age	Wonder what Mom would have thought about it?
65 Years of age	Wish I could talk it over with Mom.

A Spiritual Life

Sunday was our favorite day of the week. We loved to attend our new church that we joined. It was Camphor United Methodist Church. We have sown seeds, and God has restored our health and given us the wisdom to fulfill our destiny. He gave us dominion to do what we wanted to do. He embraced us and gave everyone an assignment.

We are members of Camphor United Methodist Church with Reverend Gloria Roach Thomas as our minister. She is very passionate, and her personality makes an ideal pastor for our church. She also has been an asset to our family, with her wisdom and her inspiration. Her sermons connect to real life situations and bring biblical lessons to life. She believes in the spirit of the church. When I was one of the ushers at Camphor United Methodist Church, I felt that greeting members with a smile provided comfort and made for a good worship service. I can say that God's plans are the best, and as you walk in His plan for life, you will experience his abundance in everything you set your hand to!

I joined Bible Study Fellowship at Christ Presbyterian Church in

Camphor United Methodist Church

Edina, and finished five years of the study. It provided me with a good base and foundation for understanding the various chapters of the Bible. When I finished the Fellowship, I felt that I really learned a great deal of knowledge and wisdom, and I was grateful for this opportunity. A favorite verse of mine is, "I can do all things through Christ who strengthens me." Philippians 4:13.

My father, Reverend Leroy Patterson, always taught us to be faithful and have courage and believe. He said, "God prepares the next chapter of our lives of more fulfillment." He loved this quote by Frederick Douglass, "You measure a man not by the heights which he has achieved, but by the depths from which he has risen." In his sermons, I liked how he related different situations to everyday life. I remembered when Dad talked about forgiveness. He said if there is a misunderstanding or serious conflict between people, there is always room for forgiveness. Some people go through years of not communicating with one another because of these misunderstandings and conflicts that have caused deep wounds. He also said that if someone has been unkind to you and you get that cringing feeling inside of you every time you see or think about him or her, then just pray about it. Dad taught me not to let unforgiveness hold me back, weigh me down, or keep me from living life. He said holding on to the hurts of your past could poison your present and limit your future. Dad said all of us would be given the grace and strength to use our whole heart to forgive. Change always begins in the heart. Choose to live the life God has prepared for you. God is good all the time.

Forgiveness can lower your blood pressure, your heart rate, and may reduce one's depression, anxiety, and anger. It is letting go of the anger of the past, and changing the future. If we are to change ourselves, then it starts on the inside with our heart. I want to be remembered as someone who taught women about their self-worth and to live their life to the fullest. Life is what you make it. Treat your brothers and sisters with dignity and love, love, love! Choose to live the life God has prepared for you. I pray for wisdom to guide my family, friends and acquaintances.

Education Never Stops

I enrolled in the University of Minnesota in 1979 for graduate work in Special Education to fulfill my purpose of teaching children with special needs. The reason I wanted to study this area is because I was thinking about when I had my first job teaching in Virginia; some of the children had behavior problems, and the teachers did not have the patience to work with them. Some of the students with behavior concerns were transferred to my classroom. I wanted to make sure children could grow and develop. For example, Joey, who had several behavioral concerns, often disrupted the other children in the classroom, and he always needed immediate attention. I set him away from the other

Markam Elementary School, 4th grade class
Joey is circled

children, who would instigate him. I worked with him to improve his behavior and attitude. He progressed so much in his learning that the principal was impressed. Right before Christmas break, Joey came to school early before the other children. He brought me a large box and said, "Mrs. Hazelwood, I have a Christmas gift for you, and I want to put this in your car." I told him to leave the box on my desk and to go out to the playground. When he left I opened the box and saw beautiful teacups and saucers that appeared to be pretty expensive. I called for the principal, and he told me that Joey's mother owned a gift shop, and that is from where the cups came. We called his mother so she could pick them up. I told Joey that my gift from him was to study hard in his reading and math and to earn gold stars on his assignments.

In order for a student to earn a gold star, he or she would have to earn between 92%-100% and for a silver star he or she would have to earn between 80%-91%. After a few months of praise and encouragement he blossomed into a very confident student.

I completed my special education degree and worked at St. Mary's Hospital in Minneapolis with chemically dependent teenagers. This was a challenging job. I had been working with elementary children before, and these students were teens in high school. I had students from all over the United States who were children of lawyers, doctors, senators, and other professions. These students had serious problems and were sent to St Mary's Hospital for treatment for six weeks. This hospital is now Fairview Riverside. I worked with these teens in algebra and reading. I also worked in the juvenile detention program in Minneapolis. This was a locked facility for teens that had committed crimes. Yes! I was uncomfortable the first day and learned not to pressure them to learn because they did not want to be in school. I worked with these students the best way I could considering their background and the locked down environment. Later I worked in the elementary schools in Bloomington with K-12.

When I studied child development in college I learned that students came from many backgrounds, and as teachers we would have to be consistent, have high expectations, and challenge students no matter what their background and baggage. There were several approaches to discipline that teachers and parents often took with their children. Three of these styles are 1) the authoritarian (demanding but not responsive, overbearing, and domineering), 2) the authoritative (demanding and responsive) and permissive (lenient, little attention, tolerant). Some of my students were from families that experienced the difficulties of divorce or experienced an abusive past. I would engage my students with challenging and interesting activities according to their personalities and academic level. I loved teaching students and taught them to respect one another. They loved my classroom and learned how to be respectful to others.

One example of a student that was raised in a bigoted home was this 14-year-old white student who said her parents did not want her to make friends with other races. She told me that her parents told her "When you go into Minneapolis, role the window up so the n------ won't come in." I asked if their family had been around children of different races. I pointed out that even if you are a different color, whether you are Black, white, Asian, or Latino, we are all the same inside, and everyone has red blood. This was quite an interesting discussion of how children are raised by parents to think the way they do. They wanted their children to think the way they did even though it was wrong. I hope by the end of the year that my 14-year-old student realized the humanity of people.

While teaching, I became an Independent Mary Kay beauty consultant. Before I started my Mary Kay business I led a busy life as wife, mother, and teacher. I always wanted to strive and reach for new goals and adventures. What inspired me to take the next step of becoming a beauty consultant was the development of relationships with many new women. As a teacher I wanted to positively influence children's lives. As a Mary Kay consultant I directly impacted the lives of women helping them to obtain the freedom and courage to dream big. When I lived in Germany I taught classes in embroidery and sewing for the Officers' Wives Club. I never thought that teaching was my calling in life. I said, "Gee whiz, I can do this", and watched the smiles on the ladies' faces when finishing a project. I am motivated to help others because when you focus more on others you feel great about yourself. We all hope to spend our lives doing what we love most, but it doesn't mean that we have to do it for a living. Whatever job moves you, it can be as rewarding as any dream job. Maybe you would like to write, paint, or play the piano, yet something is always stopping you from getting started. I had a hobby painting with oils and acrylic. I loved to paint outdoor scenery and display them in my home. I think that my goal came close to my heart's desire. Whatever obstacles there are to get you where you want to go in life, you can overcome them; just never lose faith in the path.

I was motivated to accept the Mary Kay opportunity when my independent sales director, Kalene Picotte, offered me a complimentary facial, and I was really impressed. She mentioned the Mary Kay priorities as God first, family second, and career third. I was convinced and excited about the company. Mary Kay is a way to help women embrace who they are and feel beautiful in their own skin. I loved her philosophy in sharing the opportunity to women in all phases of life.

John won a bowling award at a Mary K Conference

Mary Kay Award

Mary Kay Conference in Dallas, TX

The things that I loved about Mary Kay Cosmetics were the freedom and courage to fulfill my dreams. As I worked my business I began to flourish; my goals began to change and grow. I traded my teaching job in for teaching skin care classes to women. One of my challenges in this business was helping other women see Mary Kay as a potential flourishing business. If you dream big, don't give up, and have enthusiasm that everything will work out. Place yourself in God's hand, and everything in your life goes right. Working together and sharing ideas with other consultants was helpful. I also encouraged others and tried to instill in them that what they believe, they can achieve. Mary Kay says, "As you begin a new career, remember that whatever you vividly imagine, ardently desire, sincerely believe, and enthusiastically act upon must inevitably come to pass."

I was very successful in the Mary Kay business for over 30 years having a team of women I trained to follow their dreams. I have earned trophies of $14,000 in sales, trips to the Mary Kay headquarters in Dallas to see Mary Kay Ash, appliances, a fur coat, jewelry, china, diamonds, and lots of recognition.

Wow, what a journey! John was a great supporter making the trips to Dallas, Texas with me for seminars and conventions. There were classes for the husbands to learn about the Mary Kay business. The activities for the husbands were golf and bowling. John played golf on the first trip to Dallas. On the second trip he bowled, won the tournament, and was given a bowling pin. John enjoyed the times when I went to the bank with the "cold hard cash". He always had a smile on his face. At the Mary Kay conventions in Dallas I was amazed to find out that some of the women who became Mary Kay consultants and worked all the way to the top as national sales directors were at one time in their life doctors, nurses, lawyers, and microbiologists. They traded careers for the Mary Kay opportunity. I always would tell my consultants to work hard to fulfill their destiny, and there is no dream you can't accomplish. Now it is easy for some customers to order products on my website, and I mail whatever they ordered. Mary Kay has been a wonderful part-time business for me. I can still work on my own time, with my customers who login on my website for the updated trends in eye colors, lip colors, or skin care products.

"You cannot teach what you don't know; you cannot lead where you do not go."

Mary Kay Ash

This message is just as meaningful today as ever. It was meant for everyone. I think everyone wants to be successful in whatever they do. In shifting your focus from success to service, your work as a teacher, nurse, or doctor will quickly have more meaning. God can dream a bigger dream for you than you could ever dream for yourself. Enjoy every minute, hour, and day of your life with prayers.

Marriage

John and I celebrated our 50 years of marriage with a cruise to all of the Hawaiian Islands. We traveled to the Islands every other year previous to this year. We visited the big island of Hawaii – Maui and Oahu. This one was one of our favorite places. Yes, it is a long trip, however, we usually stop part of the way in Los Angeles to visit my sister Beverly.

July 20th, 2012, we celebrated our 60th wedding anniversary. We had a special celebration at the Fort Snelling Officers Club and rented a limousine for the day. This was a special day for us. We were apart about a quarter of those years because of John's military duties. I was the mom and dad in the

60th Wedding Anniversary & Birthday Celebration

household. There were challenges, as with any army wife, to stay connected. We had disagreements yet we always talked things over to solve them. We found that doing activities together such as golfing, bowling, and church activities made our marriage strong and lasting. My father, Reverend Leroy Patterson, said to us when we were first married that there is no such thing as a 50/50 marriage. A good marriage is 75/25, and each person gives 75%. Our long lasting marriage is the result of our perseverance and commitment to love one another. What makes a healthy union is sharing goals and growing together as a team.

Plan on the life that you want to build together, whether it's dates at fancy restaurants or relaxing weekends without the children. We loved the trips we took on cruises to Alaska and Hawaii, and the experiences kept us refreshed. The only thing about coming back from a vacation is that you have to go back to your normal routine like cooking and doing chores with no one to serve you like on the cruises. Ha-ha. You do get a bit lethargic and would like to hire a cook.

We loved packing up our RV for our long road trips to Texas and California. We would fill our refrigerator with food and pack linens and towels. We would stop at recreational parks and spend the night. One trip in our RV was to Garden Grove, California to attend Rev. Dr. Robert Schuller's church service at the Crystal Cathedral. We enjoyed watching his church service over the years, and it was a pleasure to visit and see him in person.

I loved the beautiful sights of mountains, trees, and the architecture of buildings. I would take my sketchpad and sit in the kitchen part of our RV and paint scenic places while John drove. The fall was my favorite time of the year when we were traveling west. In the mornings we would leap from the comfy bed and gaze through the window to see the beautiful foliage of brown, yellow, and red leaves. These scenes are what I like to paint using my oils or acrylic paints. I also like painting designs on glass bottles. It's a great pastime. I have some of my paintings displayed in my office and have given some away to family, and friends.

AGE

Most women are conscious about age. I can honestly say that I have never felt better. I wake up every morning rejoicing that I'm still here, with an opportunity to begin to be healthy and happy. We plan every major event in our lives; why not plan on how to age well. In the past being older than fifty, guaranteed over the hill jokes, wrinkles and the sinking feeling that life was all down hill from there. We assume that aging just happens over time, and there's little we can do about it. There are many things you can do, whatever age you are. Make sure you have a healthy diet, exercise, make sure you get at least eight hour of sleep, and manage your stress. Today the older crowd aging has never looked or felt so good. I believe we should move away from allowing our age to define who we are, what we can do, and where we fit in. Instead we should allow our minds and our attitudes to set the stage. Age is all in the mind and just a simple number and it should not determine how you should be at any particular time in your life. Our minds control our attitudes, feelings and actions. Physical health is so important and has a lot to do with age, but so does our attitude.

The New Millennium 2000 - 2013

The years of 2001 and 2002 were very eventful with sadness and joy – the 9-11 terrorist attack on the U.S, John's diagnosis, selling and moving and the death of my sisters.

9/11

This was the tragic day when the Twin Towers fell. That day of September 11 changed America forever. A plane also hit the Pentagon, and another plane crashed in Shanksville, Pennsylvania after its passengers attempted to take control of the jet from the hijackers. When this happened John and I were sitting in our living room watching TV when an announcement flashed about the disaster. It was a tragedy for America. I felt very sorrowful about the lives that were lost in this tragedy. John and I had prayed for those families and all who were involved in this sorrow. President Bush had declared September 11 a national day of service and remembrance. Even after the 10th anniversary of the tragedy there are memories, and it can never be forgotten. "Life is not measured by the number of breaths we take, but by the moments that take our breath away." said Lisa Breamer, whose husband was killed on that disastrous flight on September 11.

My sister Cora Lee moved to Minnesota in 1998 from Fort Dodge, Iowa after my father's death. We wanted her to be with her sisters here and enjoy her life. She really loved being with the family. Her nieces and nephews visited her often at her apartment. In 2001 Cora Lee passed away in the night after suffering a sudden heart attack. I recall the night before Cora passed, I went to visit her in her apartment. Our conversation was about our life in Iowa. We laughed and talked about the things we use to do. She vividly talked about how grateful she was to have wonderful parents and sisters. Cora praised everyone that was a part of her life. I am happy that I was there toward the end of her life. She loved this Bible verse, "Trust in the Lord with all your heart, and do not rely on your own understanding." She was the second of six girls.

Parkinson's Disease.

John was diagnosed with Parkinson's disease in 2001. This was a new beginning for John for God spoke to him and said, "Never give up, and let me in. You can't give up as a caregiver with such loving and dedicated spouse. We continued traveling at this time, mostly to Hawaii each year. In 2007 we took our last trip to Hawaii for his disease was

Struthers Parkinson's Center

progressing. John had the muscle rigidity in Parkinson in which sometimes it makes difficulty sitting and standing. We prayed, and the Lord answered our prayers and guided us to excellent physicians and nurses to care for John. He attended Club-Create at Struthers Parkinson's Center in Golden, MN, a therapeutic program for Parkinson's patients that specialized speech therapy, music therapy, occupational and physical therapy, along with Tai Chai and other activities. Attending the Club Create for five years greatly improved his quality of life. His smile would light of my life. I loved going there to see how John progressed.

In August 2012, I attended a program that Club Create presented. To start out the program the group did stretching exercises with the song, "Over the Rainbow". The movements of the participants were very impressive when you realized how restricted there bodies were. Before the program, John's group created a song talking about Parkinson's and how it will not defeat them. The working title, "Our Fight", which was a CD individualized to have each client's name on it. John's own personal story of being an Army Colonel came through with his contribution. His quote in the song stated, "If we gather our forces, moving forward we'll go." The chorus lyrics of "Get out of the house, Now, Now, Now" was verbalized loudly by him. His faith was evident in the lyrics, "I still have my faith. The CD was presented as "Colonel John's Fight" to the family of Colonel John Hazelwood by Club Create Music Therapy.

Even though John was very dependent on me, he still had a very independent mind. He still made a lot of important decisions and continued to do certain tasks like helping me to pay the bills and organizing our tax return. John learned to ask for help in certain tasks for things he could not do on his own. We strengthened our marriage by working together. I felt that living with advanced Parkinson's, John was so brave in fighting the battle. I had to reach out, have strength, face fear, for unconsciously I felt that the day was coming when I would be without John. John's doctor and nurse worked in this program. John attended Club Create twice a week from 9 to 3pm. He made so many friends and loved to go there. His nurse would always mention that John would give speeches about his military career. John also shared the book he wrote, "Magnificent Dreams" with his group at the center.

Habiba & John

At home I hired health aids from private agencies, to work for me during the day and night. One particular aide, Habiba, cared for John for five years. She was a committed and dedicated worker. She was there everyday rain or shine. She was so congenial and patient. Having Habiba with us was so easy because John enjoyed her company. He made her laugh all the time with his jokes and witty personality and famous sayings like, "Keep your ducks in a row".

One funny story I remember is when John was feeling his face and said he needed a shave. Habiba replied, "I shaved you two days ago" and John said, "I put fertilizer on and it grew back." That was hilarious and we just cracked up! Jackie, Brenda, and Robbie helped out on weekends. Dealing with Parkinson's was difficult for John. It was extremely frustrating to not have control of his body because of Parkinson. He could not do the things he used to do. However, John continued to be kind, courteous and in good spirit. He never complained to us. The only time we found out something was wrong was when he talked to his doctors.

God granted my husband, John, 85 years of full living and a long wonderful life until his homecoming, October 27, 2012, after a long battle with Parkinson's disease. It's very difficult for me to imagine that I have lost someone near and dear to me. His physical absence makes me face the truth that John is gone forever. John meant many things to me; husband, my provider, my safety security, my dancing partner, father of my children, grandfather, great grandfather. Our bond will continue to endure throughout my life. I am blessed with what I had with John and I will cherish our memories forever.

In 2001 we sold our beautiful Spanish home that we built after John retired from the Pentagon in Washington, D.C. It was located at 8010 Tierneys Woods Road in Bloomington, Minnesota. This was a huge event for us. We really loved this home, especially the whirlpool located in the center of the home. We lived at this location for 12 years. One day Brenda mentioned to us about a co-op being built a block from their house. We found out that this could be a unique lifestyle for us. Our home sold very quickly. We sold our recreational vehicle, too, and I felt very sad about having to downsize.

We bought a new home called Summerhill Cooperative. It was located in Bloomington, and we liked the plans. Summerhill Cooperative was newly built when we moved in. It has been designed with special features like spacious kitchens, formal dining rooms, and generous storage. Other features are an entertainment room, heated underground parking, and a car wash. Our home at Summerhill was spacious (2,300 square feet), very scenic with 18 windows. We had the opportunity to pick out our rugs and appliances because this was the time the co-op was being built. We moved in our newly built home early in 2002. This was our 15th move, and we had to downsize our furniture. We had a piano and a Genie organ, and had to make a decision about which one we would keep. John loved to play songs on the Genie organ. His favorite was "Somewhere My Love". We would play together for fun as a duet. Well, we decided to keep the piano, and the person who bought our home wanted to buy the organ. It was a hard decision. One good thing is that we love our wonderful new lifestyle in Summerhill. Our special moment is sitting in the kitchen viewing the beautiful elm, and cottonwood trees. From season to season the leaves change colors. We enjoy traveling, spending time with family and friends, or simply enjoy being at home reading and

Summerhill Cooperative

listening to music. We don't have to worry about mowing and maintaining the yard in the summer, or shoveling the snow in the winter. We have learned to love the co-op living.

President Of The United States (POTUS)

In 2008 a new president of the United States was elected. The special thing about the 44th U.S. president was that he was an African American. His name is Barack Obama. That night America made history. President Obama said, "I don't think that I am all that different actually. The things that led me to run for office like trying to figure out how to create an economy where everybody's got a fair shot and if you work hard, you can achieve your dreams. I'm still passionate about."

First Lady Michelle Obama is a very compassionate woman. She tours around the world teaching and lecturing to children about being physically fit and healthy. Her program "Let's Move" is about changing lifestyles. She visits schools, which have made significant changes due to the program. First Lady Michelle stated, "As women we must stand up for ourselves." As women, we must stand up for each other. As women, we must stand up for justice for all."

Some military families have had difficulty finding jobs after they retire. The First Lady and Dr. Jill Biden, the Vice President's wife, have supported service men and women returning from a decade of conflict in Iran and Afghanistan as their official cause. This is a cause that is dear to my heart because I am a military wife and have gone through similar sacrifices as military families of today. They have fought for the rights and freedom for us. Most Americans don't have a clear idea of the sacrifice these men, women and their families have made. In the US there has been about 2,000 companies training veterans or military spouses for jobs. Vets are taught how too apply their unique skills they have learned in the military. Today there are about 125,000 or more veterans unemployed. Mrs. Obama and Mrs. Biden are educating companies about the skills and knowledge that service members can help with. My son John Jr. served in the US Air Force as a Captain for five years. He transferred his valuable military skills to the workforce and he has a great job.

As a military spouse I taught in the schools for 1 to 3 years depending on John's assignment. I was fortunate enough to get jobs at most of the areas where John's new assignments were. However, military spouses finding jobs easily is not the general case. For many military spouses who had a hard time finding work, it was because employers were reluctant to hire employees they knew would be moving on in a couple of years due to the frequent movement of military families. In 2013 The Military Officers Association (MOAA) ran a survey. This would share their difficulty and experiences of employment for spouses. They use results to highlight the challenges of employment and career advances. The results led to more effective programs that addressed the employment and career challenges that military spouses face. Michelle Obama and Jill Biden have been addressing this issue well by taking part in the White House initiative Joining Forces: Taking Action to Serve America's Military Families.

In 2013 I watched the 2nd inauguration when President Barack Obama was sworn in. History was made again. The two bibles he had were, from Dr. Martin Luther King and Abraham Lincoln. My husband John supported him and would have been thrilled with excitement. He said in his speech, "What binds a nation, not the color of our skin. All men are created equal. Freedom is the gift of God. One thing you learn in this job is that even if something is not your fault, you're still responsible. That's how it should be."

2010 and 2011

In October 2010, James and Janelle Ball were married.

In 2011, the Lord called Evelyn, my oldest sister, on New Year's Day. When you actually lose a loved one, the after effects can be difficult. I have so many great thoughts about her. Evelyn was an organist at church and at so many events all of her life. We would sing along with the melodious tunes she played, which were inspiring to us.

In 2011, four grandchildren were married – Marcus and Stephanie in April, Jeremy and Theresa in May, Patrick and Amanda in July and Matthew and Jasmine also in July.

God has many things planned for these couples' future endeavors. They are wise to recognize that the world's challenges and advances both small and large will always confront them. This is the reality they will continue to share. The path they choose will enable them to live with Truth, Faith, and Love. They will fulfill great promises for themselves, their families, and for the world. May they live productively, spiritually, and faithfully.

Sherry Franklin graduated from University of Maryland in Public and Community Health, and graduated from nursing school in 2011. She is now a registered nurse working at Children's Hospital in Washington, DC. Hurrah! "Great job, girl!"

John Jr. also finished a graduate program in Masters of Teaching at Kaplan University in 2011.

Brenda Franklin graduated from nursing school in 2012.

Amanda Hazelwood graduated from nursing school in 2013

I am amazed by the accomplishments and beauty of my children, grandchildren, and great-grandchildren. They have given me a gift of life.

My Favorite Season

When I take the time to reflect on the remarkable moments that made up my life, I realize how beautiful life really is. I would like to tell you about a single moment that really made me feel beautiful.

Fall is the best time of the year. October is my favorite birthday month, and I celebrate every day of the month. I enjoy the crisp changing of various colors – the browns, reds, and oranges are so beautiful. Also the fall brings apple cider and chili cooking on the stove, yes! I can smell it right now. Of course, football comes next, which John loves. My #1 reason I love fall is for the fashion season. The new fall jackets say, "Goodbye to warm weather, and enjoy the cold". We also enjoy going out to the orchards, picking apples to make apple pie. The pie Brenda makes is "yummy" soooo good.

I love poetry, and in my high school English class my teacher gave an assignment to choose a poem and memorize it. I picked out a poem about nature. The name of the poem was "Falling Leaves". I memorized this poem, and later when I taught school I illustrated the poem on my bulletin boards. My students painted or sketched their ideas. Teachers were impressed with the poem. My grandchildren loved this poem. This really makes me feel beautiful and reminds me of many beautiful moments in my life. This is my poem I memorized by an unknown author.

AUTUMN LEAVES

The leaves are falling, falling,

The trees are getting bare,

To me it's just appalling,

That no one seems to care,

In parks and open spaces,

In rusty heaps that lie,

and men with vacant faces,

unheading pass them by,

By numbers they keep mounting,

thousands everyday, but no one

thinks of counting before they're swept away,

to highbrows and to mystics

numbers have no appeal,

and lovers of statistics,

will know just how I feel,

but what's the use of grumbling you never know I fear.

How many leaves come tumbling,

from all the trees each year.

Family Reflections

"If you bungle raising your children, I don't think whatever else you do matters very much."

Jackie Kennedy Onassis

Colonel John E. Hazelwood

 It takes a very special woman to be a wonderful wife and mother; someone who makes you feel warm and secure; understands your secrets, your hopes, and dreams; someone who wants only the best for her family and spends a lot of time and energy trying to provide just that.

Gloria and I have been married for a magnificent 59 years. We had been separated during wartime for months and years in the early days of marriage. The most significant fact is that she adjusted to being an Army wife for the first 27 years of marriage. Gloria was both mother and father during my absence. She was very compassionate and a firm disciplinarian for the children. She had always taken pride in striving and reaching for new goals and adventures. I feel a special blessing to be part of her life. Through her love and support, she allowed me to grow and fulfill my life's dream. My life has been blessed with Gloria by my side.

John Jr. (Son)

Mom the importance of family is a value you live and are an example of. Your life is an example of a virtuous woman. You always have been the stable factor in my life. I would not be where I am if it wasn't for your steadfast love and care. You have the ability to create the kind of memories that make us laugh, reflect, and cause us to smile. You exhibited so much love, grace and character to us. That is not the only time you have shined. I love the fact that you have decided to create a family heirloom in the form of this book. I can hear your grandchildren talking already, "Remember Grandma when she..." That is the quality you have given us growing up--- great memories. They say behind every good man is a great woman. That's my mom!! Pat and I love you very much. Thank you again.

Brenda (Daughter)

I want to take this moment to share my love and gratitude to you. You have been a great example of commitment, courage and fortitude. You have been through so much for the past few years, but through it all you have stayed strong and positive. Being a wonderful wife, mother, and grandparent. You're not only my mom, but also my best friend. We've shared some extreme lows (dad's hospitalizations) and some fabulous highs together (birthday celebrations, shopping, and vacations). With the love of God and strong family support, we have and will continue to make it through. God is good, All the Time!

Jack and I celebrated 30 years of marriage in August 2012. We plan to be just like you and dad, celebrating over 60 years.

Jeremy (Grandson)

 My full name is Jeremy John Hazelwood. I was born as the oldest of nine children, on May 25,1982. Being the oldest was easy, but I quickly realized that I either set a good or bad example for the younger siblings. They watched every move that I made. I was a quiet and introverted individual in my younger years, and am still a somewhat a calm and collected person today. I was very adventurous and often found myself venturing out into the woods beyond my backyard. I would build shelters for wildlife or whatever was out there. I would catch snakes and frogs and bring them back to the house as pets. When I

came back from the woods one day with ticks all over me that ended my interest in exploring the woods further.

In middle school I took interest in playing the drums. I was pretty good at it and eventually played in my high school band as a freshman. I got into sports my sophomore and junior year, and played soccer and basketball. As a junior I decided to go to the career center to learn how to become an electrician. It seemed like a very interesting field to go into, and I enjoyed working with my hands. After high school I pursued a degree in electronics from DeVry University. I continued working in the electrical field and have developed my skills as an electrician for the past 10 years. At the present time, October 2009, I am working towards starting my own electrical and Communications Company. The company name that I came up with is Undefined Heights Electric & Communications. I am also looking to pursue a degree in electrical engineering. Currently, my focus is creating a better life for my beautiful daughter named JereYonna Joy Hazelwood and me.

Theresa and I were married May 20, 2011. Theresa works as an academic adviser in the College of social work at Ohio State. Thanks for writing this book for our future enjoyment. Love you!!! Grandma

Janelle (Granddaughter)

My name is Janelle Marie Ball. I am the 2nd oldest in my family, and we always had lots of fun growing up! I have always enjoyed doing everyone's hair, so I became a Cosmetologist! Some of my favorite things to do are singing, baking, shopping and especially just being around my family! I married my amazing husband James R Ball III in October of 2010. It was an awesome moment! We live in Indianapolis, Indiana and enjoy traveling, trying out new restaurants, and staying in to watch movies!! My dream was always to own a salon, and that dream transpired into starting my mobile salon and spa business in 2012 called J Marie Designs LLC! I look forward to continuing to pursue my salon business, and excited about the many blessings God has in store for our family!

Marcus (Grandson)

My name is Marcus Alan Hazelwood and I am the third oldest in my family. I married Stephanie McKeel on April 30, 2011. I love playing soccer, traveling, and spending time with his family.

I work in the engineering field currently as an Energy Analyst with an engineering firm. I am certified with United States Green Building Council as a LEED AP (Leadership in Energy and Environmental Design Accredited Professional) with a specialty (BD+C) in Building Design plus Construction. I manage the designs of commercial building projects to decrease environmental pollution, reduce operating costs, and enhance community socialization.

Matthew (Grandson)

My name is Matthew Levi. I am the fourth oldest. I married my high school sweetheart Jasmine Hazelwood July 9, 2011, on a sternwheeler boat in Marietta Ohio. We are in the process of building our first home. We enjoy going out with other couples to dinner and other activities. Jasmine is currently working as a Marketing Coordinator, and a part time Cosmetology instructor. I am currently starting a new job as a Service Technician at ComDoc Inc. I will be servicing printers and copiers. This new job is more like a career as I will be able to go back to school and earn my degree paid for by the company. I eventually want to become a systems analyst and grow within ComDoc. Some of my hobbies include playing in basketball and soccer leagues throughout the year. In the near future Jasmine and I plan to start a family and fill the newly built house with children and pets!!

Patrick (Grandson)

 My name is Patrick James Hazelwood number five in the family. In May of 2010 I completed my second year of college at Malone University. I enlisted in the Army National Guard. I went to Basic Combat Training and Infantry School in Fort Benning, Georgia. After my training I served in Afghanistan for a year. I was promoted to Sargent and now I work for a unit that focuses on weapons of mass destruction.

I plan to finish my Bachelor's degree in Criminal Justice and I also plan to take an officers training course to become an officer and continue on a career in the Army. Also I've always enjoyed being involved in anything that has to deal with sports and music.

Amanda and I got married on May 14, 2011. We were married in Columbus, Ohio at the Hazelwood's home. My dad who is a part time minister officiated the ceremony. My family and friends attended, after just planning the whole thing in ten days. Amanda graduated with her LPN. Amanda hopes to finish her Bachelor's as well in Nursing. She eventually wants to work in Obstetrics or with Pediatrics. Her dream job is to work on an OB floor, and then on the side teach new mothers about the development of their baby's and what to expect when they bring their baby home.

Our future plans are to move to Columbus for a while. We will just see where God takes us. We love you Grandma!!!

Leanna (Granddaughter)

I am Leanna and I am the sixth of nine in the family. I reside in Indianapolis, Indiana. I graduated from Eastland Career Center and received my cosmetology license in May of 2010. At the Career Center, I was involved in a leadership program, called the "Stars" program and I was an Honor Roll student. I absolutely love my job as a stylist at Great Clips. With my passion for children my ultimate goal is to become an Elementary Teacher. I am now studying at Otterbein University. Grandma is proud of my goal of teaching for she also was a teacher. Besides doing hair, in my spare time, I enjoy reading, cooking, and spending time with family and friends. I enjoy volunteering with local organizations, baking, and spending quality time with my big family. I am blessed with a great family.

Andrea (Granddaughter)

Hi my name is Andrea Nicole Hazelwood. I was born on April 11, 1994. I am a freshman in high school at Pickerington Central. One of my favorite things to do is run. I love track and field. I enjoy doing hurdles and long jump. I also would love to go to college and compete in track and field. I play the flute and am in the Pickerington Tigers Marching Band. I like it so far. Other sports I enjoy are volleyball, basketball, and soccer. I also love to listen to music. I like to listen to all types of Christian music. When I am older I would love to rescue animals. I love dogs and other animals so I would like to help as many animals as I could. Currently, I am studying education at Central Ohio Technical College.

Andrew (Grandson)

Hi my name is Andrew Thomas Hazelwood, the eighth child and last boy in the family. My parents are John and Pat Hazelwood. I have four brothers and four sisters all of them are older except for one sister. I attend Pickerington High School. I paly football for the Panthers! At church, I am part of AXIS, a citywide program. This is a leadership program that prepares leaders through God and teacher participants to serve the community. Only a handful of youth were selected to for this program. I plan to join the National Guard, attend Basic Training and hopefully attend a technical college for my degree. I'm very excited for my future and I trust God that everything will work out in His way! Thank you grandma for your love and kindness.

Daneen (Granddaughter)

 My name is Daneen Naomi Hazelwood and, yes, I am the youngest child of nine in my family. My favorite color is neon purple, and my favorite animal is a panda. One thing that I have always dreamed of was to go to Spain and just go on an adventure. I also love to dance to hip-hop and Christian rap. I dance on the dance team at my church. I love to run track at my school. I enjoy running the hurdles. In the future I want to be a pediatrician. I think it would be a good thing to help children. Thank you grandma for letting me write in your book and thank everyone for reading this.

Sherry (Granddaughter)

 My name is Sherry Franklin. I was born and raised in Bloomington, Minnesota. Growing up, I was a busy girl. I enjoyed singing, modeling, playing the piano, and figure skating. I dedicated a lot of my time to the ice rink. Over the years I competed and worked hard to pass my skating tests.

I also worked hard in school. When I entered high school my main academic goal was to do well so I could go to school out east. I was accepted into the University of Maryland and attended from the fall of 2003-2007. I earned a B.S. in Public Health.

I live and work in Washington, DC. I am going back to school at Montgomery College to get my nursing degree.

In my free time I take pleasure in doing yoga and shopping. I enjoy the east coast, however, my ultimate goal would be to move out west to northern California or maybe HAWAII! (and this is how I know I am Gloria Hazelwood's granddaughter!)

Robert (Grandson)

I'm Robert Brandon Franklin, son of Jack and Brenda Franklin. I live in Bloomington, Minnesota. I love the wintertime in Minnesota; it makes me appreciate summer so much. I am one of the grandchildren of John and Gloria Hazelwood. I graduated from High School at Minnehaha Academy in 2008. After high school I attended North Park University in Chicago, Illinois. After my first year I came home to attend Normandale Community College to study Business Management. I work at the YMCA in the area of youth development. I also work as a referee and coach for youth sports. I teach the kids the fundamentals and basic skills of various sports. I also work in childcare for the Eden Prairie School district during the week. I am always around to help out my grandma and grandpa. It's nice that they live less than five minutes from the house so I can always see them. Currently, I am attending Hennepin Technical College for Computer Numeric Control (CNC) Machining to become a machinist. Machining is the automation of machine tools operated by precisely programmed computer commands. This is a great career choice for me.

Family Tree
&
Photos

Family Tree

LeRoy Patterson ————

Evelyn   Cora Lee   Jeannette

Lynn
Pamela
Mark
Annette

John ————

Patricia ——— John Jr.

Jeremy Janelle Marcus Matthew Patrick Leanna Andrea Andrew Daneen

Jere' Yonna

Jeremy ——— Theresa   James ——— Janelle   Marcus ——— Stephanie

Jere' Yonna

Matthew ——— Jasmine   Patrick ——— Amanda

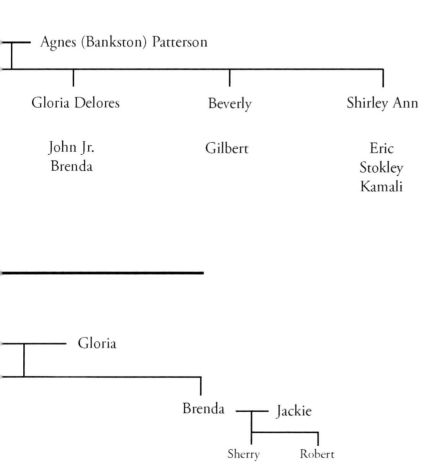

Agnes (Bankston) Patterson

Gloria Delores   Beverly   Shirley Ann

John Jr.   Gilbert   Eric
Brenda   Stokley
                                         Kamali

Gloria

Brenda — Jackie

Sherry   Robert

Agnes Patterson
(Gloria's mother)

Gloria

Four Generations

Rev. Leroy Patterson
(Gloria's father)

Agnes, Gloria, Brenda & Sherry

Family Photos

Reverend LeRoy & Agnes Patterson

60th Anniversary Wedding
Celebration

Agnes, Cora Lee, and LeRoy Patterson

The Family at church Fort Dodge, Iowa

50th Wedding Anniversary

Wedding Reception

In front of dad's ragmop car in
Fort Dodge, IA

Jeffy, Jim, John, Gloria, Nancy, Jean

Let's smile for a change

A fun cruise

Let's take a ride!

Enjoying a cruise

Virgil and John at Janelle's wedding

Enjoying Hawaii

Bowling Tournament
with Born Again Jokes
(BAJ)

John

What else do you want from the store?

Shopping in Hawaii

113

Let me think about it.

Siblings - Jim, Harriet, John

Janet and James Hazelwood

Brothers - Jim & John

James (Chink) Hazelwood Jr.
(Nephew)

James Jr. & John in uniform

Denny (Nephew)

Rodney (Nephew)

Gladys Hazelwood (Niece)

Gail Hazelwood (Niece)

Evelyn Russel
(Gloria's Sister)

Evelyn loved the piano.

Cora Lee
(Gloria's Sister)

Cora Lee & Stokley (Nephew)

Jeannette
(Gloria's Sister)

Lynn Gates

Pamela Gates

Annette Gates

Mark Gates

119

Shirley (Titilayo) Williams

Eric Williams (Gloria's nephew)

The Hazelwoods with Mahmoud El-Kati

Stokley Williams (Gloria's Nephew), Sylvia,
Aaliyah & Arie

Kamali & Shirley (Titilayo)

Beverly
(Gloria's Sister)

Gilbert (Gloria's Nephew)

Gilbert & Beverly

122

Janelle, Robbie, & Kamali

John, Gloria, Larry, Jackie & Brenda

Pat & John's Family

Pat and John

Andrew Hazelwood

Andrea Hazelwood

Leanna Hazelwood

Daneen Hazelwood

James & Janelle

Jeremy & Theresa
Hazelwood

Jere' Yonna

126

Marcus & Stephanie
Hazelwood

Patrick & Amanda Hazelwood

Matthew & Jasmine Hazelwood

Brenda and Jackie

Robbie & Sherri

The Franklin Family - Robbie, Brenda, Sherry, & Jack
Motor-Cross in Hawaii

The Franklin Family - Robbie, Brenda, Sherry, & Jack

Hazelwood & Franklin Family Reunion in Ohio

Ohio Family Reunion
Gail, Brenda, Gladys
Helen & Ruthie

Class Reunion 1948 - John, Gloria, Adeline & Dick

Gloria & Janelle

Brenda, John Jr., John & Gloria